Leader's Guide

MW00721379

BE SKILLFUL

Warren W. Wiersbe

Leader's Guide prepared by
GARY WILDE

Six Reproducible Response Sheets are
included in a removable center section.

VICTOR BOOKS

A DIVISION OF SCRIPTURE PRESS PUBLICATIONS INC.
USA CANADA ENGLAND

1 2 3 4 5 6 7 8 9 10 Printing / Year 99 98 97 96 95

ISBN: 1-56476-458-3

VICTOR BOOKS
A division of SP Publications, Inc.
1825 College Avenue, Wheaton, Illinois 60187

Before you start flipping through this Leader's Guide, stop for a couple of minutes and read pages 3–6. These pages will:
- Tell you what you'll need to know to prepare each lesson.
- Introduce different methods of leading group interaction.
- Help you evaluate how you're doing as a group leader.

KNOW YOUR GROUP

Picture the individuals who make up your group. What do you know about them? What do you need to know to lead them effectively? Here are a few suggestions:
- Develop warm relationships — get to know group members by name. Find ways to help members get to know each other as well.
- Find out what your group members already know and what they would like to know.
- Be a good listener.
- Promote an attitude of acceptance and respect among group members.

GET READY TO LEAD

If you are a little unsure of yourself because you're leading a group of adults for the first time, then follow the LESSON PLAN outlines for each session.

Using the guided discovery learning approach, each chapter will contain at least three sections:
- *Launching the Lesson* — activities that begin focusing on group members' needs.
- *Discovering God's Principles* — creative ways to communicate Bible truth.
- *Applying the Truth* — application activities that relate Bible truth to everyday life.

Some sessions may contain additional, optional sections such as:
- *Building the Body* — icebreakers and activities to help group members build relationships.
- *Prayer Time* — suggestions for praying together as a group.

REMEMBER THE BASICS

Read the entire text and this Leader's Guide. Underline important passages in the text and make notes as ideas come to you. Note any activities in the guide that take advance planning or preparation. Follow these steps in planning each session:

- Make a brief outline of your lesson plan.
- Formulate and *write down* all the discussion questions you intend to use.
- Note all activities and interaction methods you plan to implement.
- Gather all the materials you will need for the session.

Each session should focus on at least one, and often several, Bible truths that can be applied directly to the lives of your group members. Encourage group members to bring their Bibles to each session and use them. It's also a good idea to have several modern-speech translations on hand for the purpose of comparison.

USE A VARIETY OF INTERACTION METHODS

Response Sheets

Several Response Sheets are provided for you in the removable center section of this guide. Response Sheets are designed to extend the lesson's impact.

The Response Sheets in this guide will help you enliven your sessions and encourage group involvement. They are numbered consecutively *(Response Sheet 1 — Response Sheet 6)* and show with what sessions they should be used. The guide gives specific directions for when and how to use each Response Sheet in the lesson material.

Brainstorming

Announce the question or topic to be "stormed." Group members may make as many spontaneous suggestions as possible, not waiting to be called on. Don't allow anyone to criticize the suggestions. List suggestions on a chalkboard or poster board; when all are in, have the class evaluate the ideas. This method loosens up the group, involves nonparticipants, and produces new insights.

Group Bible Study

Each person should have her or his Bible open. Ask questions that will help the group learn what the passage you are studying says. Encourage sharing of insights as the group discusses the interpretations of the passage and its application to current needs. Always summarize findings. This method makes group members think; it shows them how to study the Bible on their own and it increases participation and involvement.

Discovery Groups

Divide the group into small groups of three to six persons. Appoint a leader for each group or let groups select their own leaders. Assign a topic to each group. Several — or all — groups may discuss the same topic if necessary. Allow five to eight minutes for discussion in the groups, then reconvene and get reports from group leaders. Jot findings on a chalkboard or poster board for discussion. Since many persons are freer to express themselves in small groups, this method provides maximum participation opportunity.

Role Play

Two or more group members, without advance notice or written scripts, act out a situation or relationship. Give them directions as to the kind of people they are to represent and the situation in which they find themselves. They speak extemporaneously. This method helps people "feel" situations, gives them opportunity to try different solutions, and creates interest in the lesson.

Skit

Have members read the parts of a brief script that highlights a point, provokes discussion, or presents information. Skits provide sessions with stimulating variety.

Dyads

Like *Discovery Groups*, except that there are only two people, sitting next to each other, in each "group." (If a person is left out in the pairing off, assign him to one of the twosomes.) This method makes it easy for shy persons to participate.

Discussion

In discussion, members interact not only with the group leader but with one another. Usually discussion is started by the group leader's asking a question to which there is more than a single acceptable answer. A member will respond to a question, someone else may disagree with him, and a third person may have additional comments. The leader is responsible for starting the discussion, keeping it "on track" by asking leading questions as necessary, and summarizing it after contributions cease. If a discussion gets out of hand and rambles, much of its value is lost.

Here are a few guidelines for leading discussion:

■ Maintain a relaxed, informal atmosphere.

- Don't call on people by name to take part unless you are sure they are willing to do so.
- Give a person lots of time to answer a question. If necessary, restate the question casually and informally.
- Acknowledge any contribution, regardless of its merit.
- Don't correct or embarrass a person who gives a wrong answer. Thank him or her; then ask, "What do the rest of you think?"
- If someone monopolizes the discussion, say, "On the next question, let's hear from someone who hasn't spoken yet."
- If someone goes off on a tangent, wait for him or her to draw a breath, then say, "Thanks for those interesting comments. Now let's get back to . . ." and mention the subject under consideration, or ask or restate a question that will bring the discussion back on target.
- If someone asks a question, allow others in the group to give their answers before you give yours.

EVALUATE YOUR EFFECTIVENESS

After each session, ask yourself the following questions:

_____ How well did each group member understand the lesson goals?

_____ How many group members actually took part in the lesson?

_____ Could I use other interaction methods to increase group member interest and participation?

_____ Did I nurture personal relationships with my group members?

_____ How well did I prepare the lesson?

_____ How did group members react to me as a group leader?

_____ What do I need to do to become a better group leader?

DON'T JUST MAKE A LIVING— MAKE A LIFE

TEXT, CHAPTER 1

Session Topic
By living skillfully, following the way of God's wisdom, we can make a life that will glorify Him.

Session Goals
1. To explore personal expectations for the course.
2. To discover insights about the nature and characteristics of God's wisdom.
3. To evaluate personal levels of wisdom in daily living.

Materials Needed
√ Bibles, paper, pencils
√ Copies of *Be Skillful* for each group member
√ Photocopies of *Response Sheet #1* for everyone
√ Chalkboard and chalk, or newsprint and markers
√ Optional: index cards, small pieces of candy

Special Preparation
1. Prepare for the course by memorizing a key verse: Proverbs 1:7. Try to make these words part of your thoughts each day.
2. Be ready to share some of your favorite proverbs from sources outside the Book of Proverbs. For further background preparation, read through biblical proverbs that are also found in books other than Proverbs. (For example: see the suggestions in footnote 3 at the end of the Wiersbe chapter.)

Launching the Lesson   *(20 minutes)*

Since your group is likely meeting for the first time, begin in a way that helps everyone get acquainted. After introducing yourself and handing out copies of *Be Skillful* (if you have not done so during the week), ask: **What is your worst-case experience of getting yourself lost? How did you find your way back home?**

After talking together—and laughing—about some of the responses, invite everyone to turn to the first chapter of *Be Skillful.*

Have everyone follow along as you read aloud the first two paragraphs about being lost and having a "spiritual radar" (the Holy Spirit, who guides us into truth). Then say: **The author states that we are beginning a "spiritual pilgrimage" through Proverbs. As you envision how you hope to be challenged and changed during this journey, what specific expectations do you have?** Allow plenty of time for people to talk about what they hope to study and learn in the course. Be ready to clarify course content, but also jot notes for your own review as you prepare for future sessions.

OPTIONAL: Instead of just asking the question about being lost, add some fun by handing out index cards and asking everyone to jot their answers to the question about their worst experience of being lost. Then gather the cards and shuffle them before reading them aloud. Ask group members to guess, each time, whose experience you are reading. Award a "prize" (such as a chocolate Kiss candy) for correct guesses. Follow up by reading aloud the opening paragraphs of chapter one, as described above.

Discovering God's Principles   *(25 minutes)*

Let people know that the key to grasping this first chapter is to be able to answer the author's five questions about the Book of Proverbs. Make paper and pencils available and assign the five sub-head-questions to individuals, pairs, or small groups, depending on the number of participants. Tell each group that the task is to be prepared to answer these three questions related to their section of the text. (Write these questions on the chalkboard in advance.)

- *What are the key points raised in this section?*
- *What is the most important insight that comes through to you?*
- *What key question seems to invite further exploration?*

When groups appear to be finished with their text-search and discussion, ask them to share their responses with the whole group.

If you have extra time, follow up with some or all of these discussion questions, related to the themes found under the five subheads:

1. What is the major theme of the book?
   - *Wiersbe states that wise people look at the world through the grid of God's truth. In your experience, what are some of the practical results of this approach to life?*
   - *What does it mean to deal with an adversity "successfully"? Give an example from your experience or observation.*

2. Who wrote the book, and how is it written?
   - *Clever sayings are like burrs that stick in our minds. Share one of your favorites.*
   - *Wiersbe states that "what Solomon wrote is more like a kaleidoscope than like a stained glass window." What did he mean? What special challenges and benefits does this bring to us as we read the Proverbs?*

3. What is the key verse that helps "unlock" the book?
   - *Do you agree or disagree with this statement from the text: "The way we treat our Bible is the way we treat God"? Explain your response.*
   - *When was the last time that you were clearly aware of living in "the fear of the Lord"? What characterized your attitudes and actions?*

4. What does Proverbs say about Jesus Christ?
   - *What words or phrases in the description of wisdom (in Proverbs 8:22-31) make you think of Jesus?*
   - *In your opinion, does Wiersbe see any contradiction between the "laws of nature" and the "laws of God"? How does "scientific law" fit in?*

5. What must we do to get the most out of this book?
   - *How would you distinguish the curious person from the serious one, in light of this statement from the text: "The Holy Spirit teaches the serious, not the curious?"*
   - *Why is it so important to keep in mind that the Proverbs are*

generalized statements of what is usually true in life (rather than hard-and-fast promises for all situations)?

Applying the Truth   *(15 minutes)*

Distribute copies of *Response Sheet #1* and invite your group members to consider the amount of wisdom they feel they are exercising in their lives right now. Point out that everyone is aware of areas in their lives that call for an increase in wisdom.

Most of us are also aware of ways that we stumble and fail as we continue to grow spiritually. Do encourage humor as people grapple with the concept of WQ—sometimes we are all a bit spiritually "idiotic," in light of painful past experiences of ignoring God's truth.

When everyone has chosen a WQ number, ask volunteers to describe why they chose their particular wisdom-quotient number. When several have responded, move on to the two application parts of the handout.

Allow plenty of time for people to review the chapter and jot down some wisdom qualities that appeal to them. Then ask everyone to jot at least one kind of wisdom-improvement they would like to develop in their lives.

Let people know that they will not have to reveal their ideas for improvement; it's just good to write a specific goal—one that they can review during the week in their quiet time. Close in prayer for increased wisdom during the weeks ahead.

ASSIGNMENT

Help group members prepare for the next session by encouraging them them to think about the theme: hearing the call of wisdom. Tell them that next week you'll be launching the lesson by asking these two questions:

1. When in your life did you fail to hear something important—and it made a significant difference?
2. What kinds of "internal noise" tend to keep you from "hearing" God in your spiritual journey?

IS ANYBODY LISTENING?

TEXT, CHAPTER 2

Session Topic
Hearing the call of wisdom, we cannot remain neutral, for it presents us with the choice either to accept or reject God's grace.

Session Goals
1. To consider what internal noises might hinder the hearing of wisdom's call.
2. To discover and summarize principles of wisdom in the areas of salvation, money, and decision-making.
3. To apply the concept of "either/or choosing" to a potential future problem situation.

Materials Needed
✓ Bibles, paper, pencils
✓ Copies of *Be Skillful* for each group member
✓ Chalkboard and chalk, or newsprint and markers
✓ A portable cassette player and music tape

Special Preparation
To better prepare yourself for the rest of the course, obtain a copy of a topical Bible that can help you categorize the Proverbs under thematic headings. An excellent resource for this purpose would be: *God's Wisdom for Daily Living: Every Verse in Proverbs Topically Arranged* (Nashville: Thomas Nelson, 1984).

Launching the Lesson   (15 minutes)

Begin this session with a little humor: Wear a portable cassette player into the room, earphones in place, with a music tape playing loudly enough so that people can hear some of the "overflow." Then start some small talk with group members, asking about their week, the weather, etc. When you receive responses, though, just answer: **Sorry, can't hear you. . . . The music's too loud.** Do this a few times, until people get the idea that you are having some fun with the theme of this session. Remove the earphones and ask: **How did that little demonstration illustrate the author's point in the introductory paragraphs of the text?** After people share their ideas, generate deeper discussion about the topic by asking:

- *When in your life did you fail to hear or notice something important — and it made a significant difference?*
- *What kinds of "internal noise" tend to keep you from "hearing" God in your spiritual journey?*

Discovering God's Principles   (30 minutes)

Now direct attention to Proverbs 1:8-9, and point out that hearing and living by the wisdom of God is like putting on fine jewelry. Then say: **There are three "gem statements" that sparkle with important truth for us in this chapter of Wiersbe's text. As I jot them on the chalkboard, try to find them in your texts.** This will be an opportunity for everyone to quickly review the chapter. You will be writing these three statements on the board:

Under subhead #1 (Salvation): "The message of God's truth is made for the marketplace, not the ivory tower."

Under subhead #2 (Money): "It's good to enjoy the things that money can buy, provided you don't lose the things that money can't buy."

Under subhead #3 (Decisions): "The better you know God, the keener will be your knowledge and discernment when it comes to the decisions of life."

Distribute paper and pencils, have people count off by three's, and assign one of the three topics to each individual. Tell group

12

members that their task is to find some of the "facets" (i.e., supporting points in the biblical passages and in *Be Skillful* explanations) that make the gem statements shine. For example: for the first statement, a supporting point might be the phrase "wisdom calls aloud in the street" (Proverbs 1:20) or Wiersbe's statement that "we must herald the word in an uncompromising way."

Allow only a couple of minutes for this exercise, then ask for reports. Follow up with these questions to the whole group:

- *Summarize your personal insights under the themes of salvation, money, and decision-making. What practical significance do these gem statements have for you?*
- *When have you felt that you obviously heeded or ignored these principles — to your benefit or regret?*

Applying the Truth   *(15 minutes)*

Begin this step by first reading aloud the last paragraph of this chapter in *Be Skillful*. Summarize Wiersbe's either/or challenge and then say: **In order to be committed to the Lord in a general, whole-life renunciation, it's good to prepare for the particular choices that we'll be facing in the coming days. For example, many counselors use a technique to help people begin to solve their problems before they happen. The counselor asks a client to consider: What will be your next crisis?**

Ask your group members to take time to consider that question for a moment, in light of the either/or statement that Wiersbe makes in the last paragraph of the chapter. Say: **Think about a tough situation you are facing now — or likely will face sometime in the future. Envision the choices that you'll confront and pick one "either/or" decision you'll no doubt have to make.**

Have your group members link up with prayer partners (or spouses) in order to talk about their next crisis and describe what *acceptance* or *rejection* of God's wisdom in that situation would actually look like for them. Allow a few minutes for partners to pray for wisdom in their future crisis scenarios.

ASSIGNMENT

Ask group members to prepare for the next session by thinking about this question: **If your life were laid out as a route on a road map, how would it look? What would be the evidence that wisdom was influencing your path's twists and turns?**

THE PATH OF WISDOM AND LIFE

TEXT, CHAPTER 3

Session Topic
When we choose to walk according to His wisdom, God responds by protecting, directing, and perfecting our path.

Session Goals
1. To identify ways of recognizing when we are on the path of wisdom.
2. To discover the biblical requirement, and rewards of following wisdom.
3. To offer thanks and praise for God's wise leading through the paths of life.

Materials Needed
√ Bibles, paper, pencils, index cards
√ Copies of *Be Skillful* for each group member
√ Chalkboard and chalk, or newsprint and markers
√ Tape, three shoe boxes (or other containers)

Special Preparation
1. Take some time to do your own life-path drawing, as described in *Applying the Truth*.
2. Highlight times of God's protecting, directing, and perfecting in your life, and be ready to talk about those times.

Launching the Lesson   *(15 minutes)*

Begin by distributing paper and pencils. Ask everyone to think of a destination that is within five miles of your meeting place and tell everyone to draw a simple map showing the best route to that destination. Stipulate that the map should show roads, but have no words—just pictures and symbols for various landmarks.

Have everyone write their names on their papers and exchange them. Then spend a few moments inviting volunteers to guess where the maps are leading them. The exercise should result in a declaration of your groups' best direction-giver or "pathfinder."

Then debrief the activity and lead into your session's topic by asking questions like these:

- *How good are you at choosing the best route to a destination?*
- *When you looked at the map handed to you, how many of you knew of a different way, a faster way, or a better way to get to a particular destination?*
- *When you are driving in an unfamiliar area, how do you tell if you are on the right road or the wrong road?*
- *How can you tell when you are on the right road spiritually? When is it hardest to tell that you are on the right spiritual road?*
- *How do you deal with those times of uncertainty?*

Say: **In our chapter's introductory paragraphs, Wiersbe states: "The only way to end up at the right destination is to choose the right road." How do you relate that statement to your experience of attempting to grow in wisdom over the years?** Encourage group members to talk about any times when they've experienced the blessing of being on the right path in their walk with God—or the pain of discovering that they had "gotten off the track" in their spiritual life. Be ready to share your own examples before moving to the *Discovering* step.

Discovering God's Principles   *(25 minutes)*

If possible, gather everyone in a tight circle (or be seated around a table), and place three shoe boxes in the center of the circle, each labeled with one of these words: REQUIREMENTS, REWARDS, RETRIBUTIONS. Make sure everyone has plenty of index cards and a pencil. Then assign the three biblical chapters (Proverbs 2,

3, and 4) to individuals and tell them their task is to read through the passages to find instances of the three Rs. Each time they find one of the Rs they should jot a brief summary of the verse or phrase — with its reference number — and toss the card in the appropriate box.

OPTIONAL: You may wish to challenge your group members to jot their Scripture summaries in paraphrase form, with modern words and circumstances substituting for ancient ones.

When you have three boxes of cards, get volunteers involved in taping them to the wall in this manner: Requirements and Rewards will form an arrow that points in a sloping, upward direction; the Retributions will form an arrow that bends downward. (Note: There won't be many cards in the Retributions box, but see: 2:18-19, 22; 3:12, 25, 32-35; 4:16-17, 19.)

Read aloud several of the entries on the cards, then direct attention to the arrows and ask: **In light of our findings about the kind of path we can choose in life, what general principle would you formulate about the path of wisdom? State your principle in one sentence that uses all three R-words, if possible.**

Give people plenty of time to think about this and to write their principles on paper. Then ask volunteers to share what they've written. Follow up with some or all of these discussion questions:

- *Wiersbe points out that "life is dangerous and it's wise to listen to the counsel of godly people who have walked the path before us." Who has been a spiritual mentor for you in this way? How did this person help you grow in wisdom?*
- *According to the text, the safest and most satisfying path is the path of wisdom. In the context of Proverbs, what does "a safe life" mean, in practical terms? In what ways has your Christian journey been safe and/or unsafe?*
- *Proverbs 3:5 tells us not to lean on our own understanding. How would you explain your way of following God's leading without, as Wiersbe says, "turning off your brain"?*
- *Do you agree with the statement that "everybody has some vision before them that helps to determine their values, actions, and plans"? How would you put your personal vision into words?*

Applying the Truth   (20 minutes)

Draw your session to a close by giving group members opportunity to consider how God's wise leading has influenced them along the pathways of their lives. Hand a sheet of white paper, along

16

with a marker or crayon, to each person.

Say: **We've spent time in our session today looking at the paths that wisdom and folly make for us. Now take some time to draw the path of your own life as you have lived it so far. On your pathway, show any or all of these journey-items:**

- crossroad decisions
- major detours
- dead-end streets
- slow turn-arounds
- straight and speedy highways
- bumpy lanes
- ruts and ditches

Write the list of items on the chalkboard and let people know that they can choose to draw the path of: (1) their whole life; (2) a significant year of their life; (3) any recent period of time. Let them know, too, that they can choose to show as many or as few of the suggested journey-items as they feel comfortable revealing.

When people are through working, ask volunteers to talk about some of the things they've drawn. Then invite everyone to go back and label the times—at least one—when they felt *protected* (Proverbs 2), *directed* (Proverbs 3), or *perfected* (Proverbs 4) by God. At the end of this period, spend time offering sentence prayers of praise and thanksgiving for God's wise leading.

ASSIGNMENT

Ask group members to prepare for next week's topic by thinking about this question: **Where, when, and how am I most vulnerable when it comes to being tempted by sexual sin?**

THE PATH OF FOLLY AND DEATH

TEXT, CHAPTER 4

Session Topic
Because God invented sex, He alone is qualified to tell us how to use it properly.

Session Goals
1. To introduce reasons for the sexual boundaries God has set for us.
2. To develop counseling approaches that could help people who struggle with sexual sin.
3. To encourage and pray for one another regarding sexual temptations.

Materials Needed
√ Bibles, paper, pencils, index cards
√ Copies of *Be Skillful* for each group member
√ Chalkboard and chalk, or newsprint and markers

Special Preparation
1. Learn about the Bible's pronouncements against various sexual sins by reading through the texts listed in the first paragraph of chapter four: Leviticus 18; Romans 1:18-22; 1 Corinthians 6:9-20; Ephesians 5:1-14.
2. In advance, place *Visual Sketch #1* on a large piece of newsprint or butcher paper.

LESSON PLAN

Launching the Lesson   *(10 minutes)*

Introduce your session by talking about a cartoon that showed Moses speaking. He had just returned from Mt. Sinai with the stone tablets of the Ten Commandments in his hands, and is reporting to the people about his encounter with God on the mountaintop. Moses announces: "It was hard bargaining—we get the milk and honey, but the anti-adultery clause stays in."

Ask: **In light of this cartoon, how would you answer a neighbor who says: "Seems like you Christians have a God who is just out to keep us from having a good time—a real celestial party pooper!"**

After fielding some responses, direct attention to the words in the second paragraph of chapter four, under subhead one: "God created sex not only for reproduction but also for enjoyment, and He didn't put the 'marriage wall' around sex to rob us of pleasure but to increase pleasure and protect it." Solicit reactions to this quote before summarizing today's session topic: **Today we're going to explore practical reasons why Wiersbe's statement is true by considering why going against God's plan for sexual fulfillment does not bring lasting satisfaction.**

Discovering God's Principles   *(30 minutes)*

Give a brief overview of the three subhead divisions in the Wiersbe chapter. Focus on the disappointments, destructiveness, and deadly consequences of sexual sin. (Note: Because sexuality is a potentially embarrassing topic for some people, proceed with care and sensitivity appropriate for the comfort range of your particular group. You as leader may also feel ill at ease leading a discussion in this area. Remember though that Scriptures deal extensively with this topic because the sexual drive is foundational to human nature. Besides, God invented it!)

Now say: **Let's do a practical exercise that will help us bring biblical principles to bear on the sexual problems people may bring to a pastoral counselor. Your job is to imagine that you are such a counselor (or part of a counseling team). Your specific task is to develop a "counseling plan," that is, an outline of the topics and concerns you'd want to cover with an individual or couple who is struggling with sexual sin.**

Hand out paper and pencils and direct attention to *Visual Sketch*

#1 (placed on the chalkboard in advance) for everyone to copy on their sheets of paper:

A Counseling Plan		
Spiritual Growth *Issues to Explore:*	Relational Conflict *Problems to Resolve:*	Emotional Healing *Challenges to Work On:*
▸	▸	▸
▸	▸	▸
▸	▸	▸
Relevant Scriptures and Wiersbe Quotes:		

Visual Sketch 1
A Counseling Plan

Be sure to let people decide whether they wish to work individually or in pairs (with spouses together). Or you may decide that the exercise could best be done in two large groups, divided by gender. Assign individuals or groups one of these counseling topics:

—a couple struggling with the aftermath of adultery
—a person dealing with lustful thoughts
—a teen coping with guilt about having premarital sex.

Tell group members that they should develop the situations as they wish and then jot their ideas under the three headings on their papers: (1) issues to raise; (2) possible counseling goals they would strive for; and (3) approaches they might use in dealing with each area. Tell them to draw on the Scriptures, the *Be Skillful* chapter, and their own life experiences for their responses.

After several minutes of silent work, re-gather as a whole group and develop consensus on some of the concerns that would need to be raised, along with the best approaches or methods to use. Then draw this step to a close with this discussion question: **In your opinion, to what extent is sexual sin the result of our unwillingness to face and feel our essential loneliness?**

Applying the Truth
(20 minutes)

Now ask for a reaction to this quote by President Jimmy Carter, in an interview, October, 1976: "I've looked on a lot of women with lust. I've committed adultery in my heart many times. This is something that God recognizes I will do—and I have done it—and God forgives me for it." After a few people respond, say: **All of us do struggle with temptation. Yet, as Wiersbe says: "We can't help being tempted, but we can certainly help tempting ourselves."**

Distribute three or four index cards to each person. Ask people to silently brainstorm ways adults do tempt themselves and have everyone write ideas on the cards—anonymously. Then collect the cards, shuffle them, and have a recorder jot key phrases on newsprint as you read the items on the cards aloud.

OPTIONAL: To give your application step more personal impact, invite each of your adults to pick the temptation for which he or she feels a particular vulnerability. They'll do this anonymously. Simply have them spread their chairs out in a large circle, facing outward, so that no one can see anyone else. Take the folded newsprint to each individual, ask them to make a star with the marker (as you turn away) next to their most troubling temptation, and have them fold it again before giving it back to you.

When everyone has had a chance to mark a star, have everyone turn their chairs facing into the center of the room (or the front), and display the temptation-marked piece of newsprint. Make this the centerpiece for your closing as people pray sentence prayers for one another to avoid sexual sin, mentioning some of the specific temptations that were marked on the sheet.

Close with a word of encouragement as people contemplate the entries on the newsprint before them, such as: **Some of us may be involved—or have been—in secret sins and struggles right now. Actually, we should assume this is true. But as we go from this place, we can be encouraged that God is always ready to start over with us as we make the decision to seek His forgiveness and forsake our sins. Remember: "If we confess our sins, he is faithful and just and will forgive us our sins and purify us from all unrighteousness"** (1 John 1:9).

ASSIGNMENT

Ask group members to be ready to share their responses to this question in the next session: **If you had to use a concrete analogy to describe the process of spiritual growth, how would you "picture" it?**

PEOPLE, WISE AND OTHERWISE – Part 1

TEXT, CHAPTER 5

Session Topic
Making a life that glorifies God requires proceeding along the path of wisdom while shunning the way of wickedness.

Session Goals
1. To highlight the contrast between making a good living and making a good life.
2. To explore the implications of pursuing wisdom or wickedness.
3. To describe and apply the spiritual growth process, in terms of purposes, problems, and progress.

Materials Needed
√ Bibles, paper, pencils
√ Copies of *Be Skillful* for each group member
√ Photocopies of *Response Sheet #2* for all participants
√ Chalkboard and chalk, or newsprint and markers

Special Preparation
Ask your pastor if you can borrow his or her favorite biography or book of church history. Read from it in preparation for this session. Be ready to share what you've learned in relation to Wiersbe's statements about the benefits of such readings.

Launching the Lesson   *(25 minutes)*

Start your session by directing attention to this quote from *Be Skillful:* "Educated and trained people who ignore or reject Christ can succeed in making a good *living,* but without Him they can never succeed in making a good *life* that glorifies God."

Hand out paper and pencils, place *Visual Sketch #2* on the chalkboard, and invite everyone to copy the sketch onto their papers.

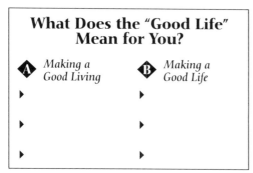

Visual Sketch 2
What does the good life mean for you?

Ask: **What does making a good living mean for you? Jot some things under each of these columns (which contrast making a living with making a life). These should be things you've done, or would like to do, or envision doing in the future.**

Give everyone a chance to think and write for a couple of minutes. Then give these directions: (1) draw arrows from entries in column A that contribute to, or foster entries in column B; (2) circle entries in column A that fight against entries in column B.

Now have everyone look again at their two columns. Say: **In light of the benefits and drawbacks of pouring so much energy into "making a good living," what would be the wisest course of action for you as you "launch" into your next five years (pick one):**

■ *Maintain course: full speed ahead;*
■ *Set a new heading: a subtle adjustment in speed or direction;*

- *All engines, full reverse: back up and/or start over in some areas.*

Invite volunteers to explain their choices and to give concrete examples, if possible. Then make your transition into the rest of the session by saying: **The Proverbs draw a distinct contrast between persons characterized by wisdom and those characterized by wickedness. Though the way of wisdom requires obedience and discipline, our text says: "The way of wisdom is the way of true life." Let's find out more about these two approaches to life. . . .**

Discovering God's Principles   *(20 minutes)*

Distribute copies of *Response Sheet #2* and briefly recap the outline of *Be Skillful,* Chapter Four. Have people fill in the numbered columns on the sheet, taking notes as you speak. Then they can refer to the sheet (before using it again in *Applying the Truth*) as a visual aid during a discussion time based on some or all of these questions:

- *How would you describe the difference between knowing about the Bible and hearing God speak through His Word?*
- *Wise people control the TV set! How are you doing in that area? What advice would you give to a parent whose children seem to be "hooked" on television?*
- *Wiersbe says: "When you fear the Lord, you keep your priorities straight." In what ways have you seen this principle operating in your life? Give specific examples, if possible.*
- *Explain how this idea from the Wiersbe text strikes you: "As we read and study Scripture, we associate with the wise men and women of Bible history and learn from them." Who are your best biblical friends?*
- *According to the text, "The self-confident person isn't wise." Do you agree? Explain.*
- *The book points out that the speech of wise people nourishes us as we listen. What are some characteristics of "nourishing speech"? When have you been nourished by someone's words?*
- *Have you found that "hard work is a thrill and a joy when you're doing the will of God"? Does this mean that when we have no joy we are not doing God's will? Explain.*
- *Wiersbe refers to the "great gift of imagination" that God has given us, out of which either evil or good is born. In your*

opinion, does the church emphasize the use of the imagination too much or too little? What wise, creative uses of the imagination could you suggest at your church in the areas of: worship, Christian education, prayer, and fellowship?

■ *God hates the sowing of discord among Christian brethren. Why is this such a devastating sin?*

Applying the Truth   *(15 minutes)*

Ask everyone to take up their *Response Sheets* again and consider the meaning of the pictured Growth Intersection. Explain: **In our study so far, we've seen stark contrast between the two ways of living: wisdom and wickedness. We know, however, that once we accept Christ we launch out on a voyage of spiritual growth that has its ups and downs — we're buffeted by some winds and waves along the way.** (Note: Ask people to share their "concrete analogies" of spiritual growth here, as suggested in last week's assignment.) **To use another biblical analogy, we are in a process of continually taking off and putting on spiritual clothes — taking off parts of the old life and putting on the new life of Christ, whose Spirit dwells within us. Though we are no longer characterized by wickedness, we may still find some wicked tendencies plaguing us as we progress toward spiritual maturity.**

Have volunteers read aloud the Scripture passages listed on the *Response Sheet.* Ask for questions or comments related to these passages and your explanation above. Then invite everyone to take a moment to fill in the Growth Intersection portion of the *Response Sheet.*

Close with a couple of minutes of brainstorming around this key application question: **When wisdom and wickedness vie for their hearts, what things help Christians make progress in their spiritual growth?**

A S S I G N M E N T

Invite your group members to prepare for the next session by thinking about this quote from chapter 6 of *Be Skillful:* "It's a dangerous thing to reject God's invitation to walk the path of wisdom and of life. You may never get another opportunity." Ask them to think about what, in practical terms, constitutes "rejecting" God's wisdom.

PEOPLE, WISE AND OTHERWISE – Part 2

TEXT, CHAPTER 6

Session Topic
By trusting in God and applying His wisdom to our lives, we can avoid the fate of the simple, the scorner, and the fool.

Session Goals
1. To explore the difference between occasional lack of common sense and the lifestyle of a fool.
2. To mark the *Be Skillful* text, based on reactions, questions, and insights.
3. To apply the principles of wisdom to contemporary issues in believers' lives.

Materials Needed
√ Bibles, paper, pencils
√ Copies of *Be Skillful* for each group member
√ Chalkboard and chalk, or newsprint and markers
√ Optional: a highlighter marker for each group member.

Special Preparation
Place the text-marking symbols on chalkboard or newsprint in advance, so you won't have to break the flow of the session by stopping to write. (You may wish to jot the symbol along with just the underlined words, as shown in *Discovering*.)

Launching the Lesson   *(10 minutes)*

Use a thought-starter question to open your session. Ask: **When in your life did you display the least common sense?** Encourage people to share stories about times when they acted wisely — or not. Start with your own story, and encourage appropriate humor, acknowledging that many of us experience occasional gaps in common-sense. Ask: **What is the difference between an occasional loss of common sense (which may get us into embarrassing situations), and the life characterized by lack of sense?** Bring out the contrast between common-sense gaffs and ongoing foolish living apart from God, as described in Proverbs.

Point out that today's session deals with the simple as those who lack "prudence or common sense" (Proverbs 1:4). We'll also be considering the scorner and the fool. Say: **Wiersbe calls these types of people the Terrible Trio, because they are: (1) naive (the "simple"); (2) filled with pride (the "scorner"); and (3) without substance (the "fool").**

Discovering God's Principles   *(25 minutes)*

Be thoroughly interactive during this step, following the discussion agenda of your group members. Here's how: First, hand out highlighter markers (or just pencils) and point to these text-marking symbols you've placed on the chalkboard (or newsprint) —

! = This gets a *reaction* from me.
? = This raises a *question* in my mind.
X = I *disagree* with this statement or idea.
" = Here's a *quote* that deserves comment.
* = There's a significant *personal insight* here.

Say: **It's up to you to generate "grist" for our discussion mill today! With your markers ready, quickly skim through Wiersbe's chapter 6 to review its content. When you come to a reaction, question, disagreement, intriguing quote, or personal insight that you want to raise for the group's consideration, mark it appropriately. This way we'll be building our discussion agenda. Be ready to report, when I call for your contributions.**

Next, after allowing people sufficient time for silently reviewing and marking, call for their responses by going through the five kinds of markings, one at a time (For example, "Who *reacted* to something in the text? How?" Or: "What *questions* came to mind?"). You should generate plenty to discuss—all related to the issues your group members want to explore.

Applying the Truth   *(25 minutes)*

Ask group members to share their thoughts about the quote assigned to them last week: "It's a dangerous thing to reject God's invitation to walk the path of wisdom and of life. You may never get another opportunity." After fielding some comments, point out that seeking to *apply* God's instructions to daily life is the opposite of *rejecting* them. Then use these discussion questions to help group members make personal applications to the themes brought out in this chapter of *Be Skillful*—

- Related to "The Simple"—*What evidence do you see that "most people today don't believe in absolutes"? How is this affecting your community's schools, neighborhoods, and law-enforcement agencies? How can Christians respond to this situation of cultural naiveté?*
- Related to "The Scorner"—*In your opinion, how much of the media criticism of Christians (or the so-called "radical right") is based on character assassination and ridicule, rather than philosophical arguments of substance? What part of this criticism is deserved? What examples of deserved and undeserved criticism can you give from TV or your local newspaper? What is a wise response?*
- Related to "The Fool"—*Wiersbe states that "God warns us that we don't know our own hearts and we can't always trust what our hearts say to us." Yet how would you describe the role of intuition in discerning God's will? How can a believer tell the difference between an inner nudge of the Holy Spirit and a case of self-deception based on whim or pride? Give an example from your own experience.*

Close in prayer.

Building the Body

This might be a good time to hold a brief open forum on: "How is our group doing?" At this mid-point of your course, you no doubt have ideas about what is working and what isn't, in terms of both learning and growing in fellowship. Others in the group have ideas along these lines too! Let them express their affirmations and concerns under three broad headings: strengths, weaknesses, suggestions. Conduct this exploration in the spirit of brainstorming about how to improve the health and functioning of your group. Accept all suggestions without judgment, until you are ready to discuss the pros and cons of each. You might cover such items as: the methods of study, the meeting time and environment, the leadership arrangement, and the level of sharing and mutual encouragement you are experiencing.

A S S I G N M E N T

Invite group members to prepare for the theme of your next session by watching the video, *Lost in America*. This humorous movie focuses on the money and work values of society and deals with the tension between our need for freedom and our desire for security.

"RICH MAN, POOR MAN, BEGGAR MAN, THIEF"

TEXT, CHAPTER 7

Session Topic
God's wisdom is more important than money, and our value to Him is unrelated to our financial position.

Session Goals
1. To explore financial attitudes by imagining having more than enough money.
2. To analyze the biblical descriptions of approaches to work.
3. To discuss personal "worth," apart from money.

Materials Needed
√ Bibles, paper, pencils, index cards
√ Copies of *Be Skillful* for each group member
√ Copies of *Response Sheet #3* for each person
√ Chalkboard and chalk, or newsprint and markers
√ Yellow construction paper, cut into check-size pieces

Special Preparation
If possible, watch the video, *Lost in America,* and be prepared to discuss it's portrayal of modern-day attitudes toward work and money.

UR WQ?*

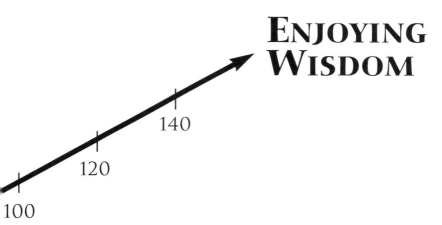

ENJOYING WISDOM

140

120

100

I would like to improve my WQ in the following areas:

_____
_____
_____
_____

I could begin doing this by:

_____
_____
_____

QUOTIENT

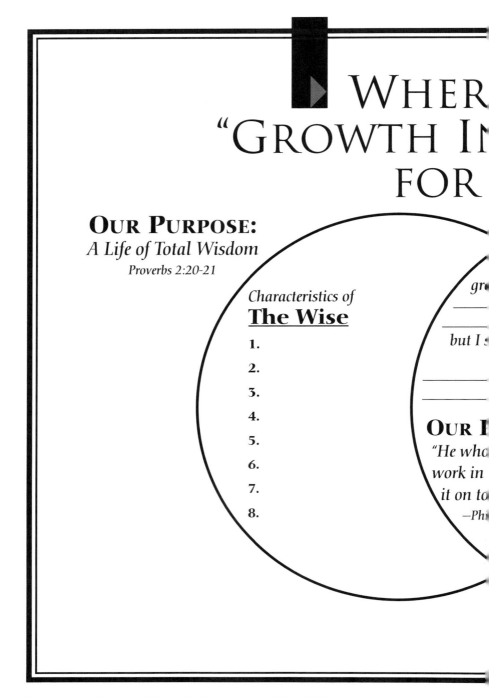

WHER
"GROWTH IN
FOR

OUR PURPOSE:
A Life of Total Wisdom
Proverbs 2:20-21

Characteristics of
The Wise

1.
2.
3.
4.
5.
6.
7.
8.

gr
_____
but I s
_____
_____

OUR F
"He who
work in
it on to
—Ph

favorite reference:

What qualities of "Diligence" would you like to display on the job?

. . . .

Favorite reference:

PART B

What is your overall attitude toward:
Work _____

Money _____

Salary Requirement: $_____

"Each of us must discover at what financial level God wants us to live and be content with it."

—*Warren Wiersbe*

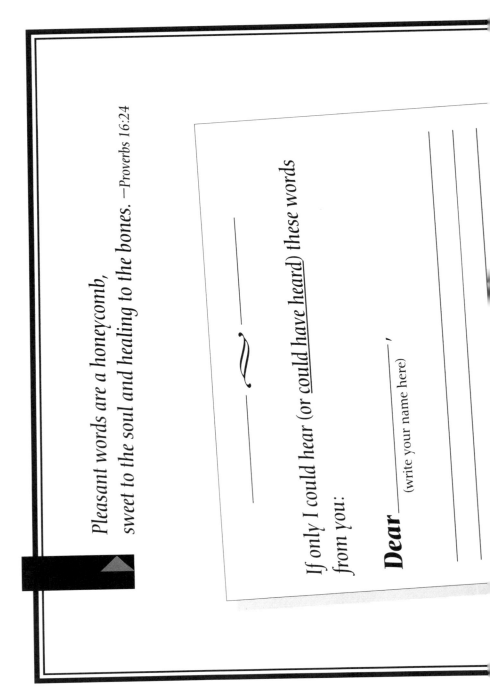

Pleasant words are a honeycomb, sweet to the soul and healing to the bones. —Proverbs 16:24

If only I could hear (or <u>could have heard</u>) these words from you:

Dear _____,
   (write your name here)

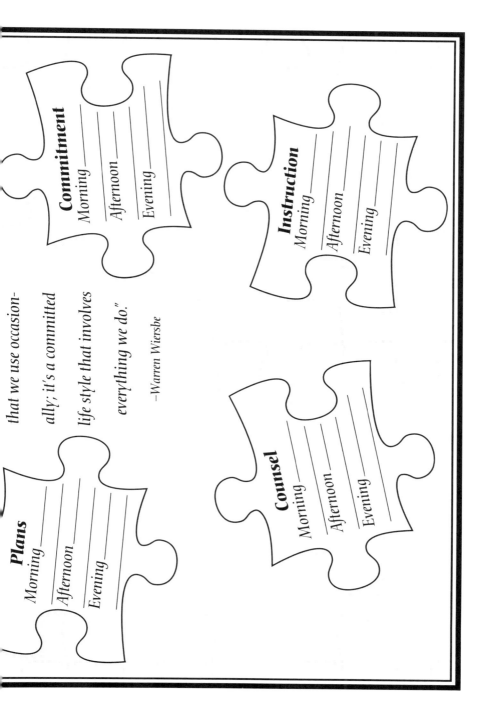

Commitment
Morning
Afternoon
Evening

Instruction
Morning
Afternoon
Evening

that we use occasion-

ally; it's a committed

life style that involves

everything we do."

–Warren Wiersbe

Plans
Morning
Afternoon
Evening

Counsel
Morning
Afternoon
Evening

THIS IS

A HOLY GOD
A time when I was awed
by God's holiness was:

_____

_____

_____

_____

A SOVEREIGN GOD
I am (or have been) keenly aware
that "God is in control" when:

_____

_____

_____

_____

The Word Became Flesh and Ma

MY GOD:

A COMPASSIONATE GOD

A time when I most need or
needed God's compassion was:

_____

_____

_____

A WISE GOD

The kind of wisdom I need
most for my future is:

_____

_____

_____

_____

His Dwelling among Us –John 1:14

GOD'S WILL—

Bringing the Pieces Together

*Trust in the Lord with all your heart and lean not on your own understanding;
in all your ways acknowledge Him, and He will make your paths straight.* —Proverbs 3:5-6

Faith

Morning _____

Afternoon _____

Evening _____

Guidance

Morning _____

Afternoon _____

Evening _____

"Knowing and doing

the will of God isn't a

Response Sheet 5. Use with Session 11 of *Be Skillful.*

Signed ,
(write another person's name here)

Think:

•What grief do I have about not hearing these words?

•What forms of acceptance or adjustment can help me move through my grief?

•What steps could I take that might restore a relationship–to make it possible for these words to be spoken to me?

APPLICATION FOR EMPLOYMENT

Position: Kingdom Worker

PART A

Do you have any of these characteristics of a "Thief or Sluggard?"

. . . .

Favorite reference:

If you are "Poor and Needy," list possible reasons:

. . .

IS THE
TERSECTION"
OU?

in

_____

_____,

ruggle

_____

_____ .

GRESS:
n a good
vill carry
pletion"
s 1:6

Characteristics of
The Wicked

1.

2.

3.

4.

5.

6.

7.

OUR PROBLEM:
Some "Wickedness" Still Mixed In
Ephesians 4:14-24; Philippians 3:12-16;
Colossians 3:4-14

WHAT'S Y

Qualities and characteristics of wisdom that appeal to me:
(Skim the chapter and jot six items that seem particularly significant to you.)

_____
_____
_____
_____
_____
_____
_____

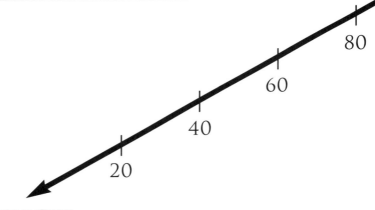

80

60

40

20

STUCK
IN FOLLY

*WISDOM

Launching the Lesson   (15 minutes)

Start by taking your group members on a fiscal flight of imagination. Say: **Just last month you entered the Publisher's Clearinghouse Sweepstakes by returning your entry form in time. Now your doorbell rings, and there is Ed McMahon, standing at your door, smiling at you, with his hand holding out a piece of paper. You take the paper and discover that it is a check made out to you, but with the amount left blank.**

Ed says: **"You've won our Grandest Grand Prize ever! Just fill in this blank check with any amount you want; we'll cover it. Enjoy!"**

As he walks away, you wonder: *Just how much would I like to have?* **You take up your pen and begin to write the amount of money you'll soon have in the bank; it's the beginning of your dreams. . . .**

As you speak, distribute pens and slips of yellow paper (roughly the size of a check). Ask group members to think about the figure they would write on the check and then have them jot it down. When everyone has written a specific figure, ask questions like these to generate a discussion about money attitudes:

- *What amount did you write? Why? (Why not more . . . or less?)*
- *What changes would you make in your lifestyle once you received this money?*
- *How would having this money likely change you? Your spouse (or other relatives)?*
- *What problems could having this money bring to you?*

Use the final question to direct attention to the last six paragraphs of *Be Skillful,* chapter 7, which describes some of the perils and problems of wealth. Then summarize by saying: **Though there's nothing inherently wrong with riches, Proverbs makes the point that God's wisdom is more important than money. Let's look at the three kinds of people described in our text and consider their relationship to work and money.**

Discovering God's Principles   (25 minutes)

Read aloud these two key verses mentioned by Wiersbe: Proverbs 16:16 and Matthew 6:33. Then say: **We work for money, but we** are working for other things, too. As members of God's Kingdom we realize that we must keep our priorities in proper order. Let's be imaginative again: What would it be like to apply for a job as Kingdom Worker? What questions might our Almighty Employer have for us, in light of His Word?

Hand a copy of *Response Sheet #3* to each individual and give these instructions: Tell people to use the Bible and the *Be Skillful* text to help them fill in the questions in Part A (this will give them a handle on the content under the three subheads). Let people know that though there are many descriptions of thieves, the poor, and the diligent, they can just choose to list any three items. For "Favorite Reference" have group members choose a Bible verse or passage that best summarizes for them the point of the text. As people move to Part B of the sheet, ask them to answer as candidly as possible; let them know that they will not have to reveal their Salary Requirement.

When everyone is through working on the *Response Sheet,* ask for a sharing of responses. Supplement participants' comments and questions with some or all of the discussion questions below.

Under "Thieves and Sluggards"
- *In what ways are dishonesty and laziness a form of thievery?*
- *What types of "get-rich-schemes" are you most tempted by? What have you learned from your own mistakes in this area — or from observing others fall prey to scams?*
- *Wiersbe asks us to recognize that "work is not a curse." When is it hardest for you to believe that? When has work been a great blessing or privilege for you?*

Under "Poor and Needy"
- *What criteria do you use in determining whether someone is "freeloading" or truly needy?*
- *If God "doesn't respect the rich more than He respects the poor," why do we tend to do so?*
- *How did you learn your work ethic? How can Christian adults today instill a strong work ethic in their young people? What aspects of our culture seem to militate against this?*

Under "Diligent"
- *Explain how the "reward" for faithful hard work (that is, more work) really is a reward.*
- *How do you, personally, determine how much credit debt is appropriate for you? How can the misuse of credit become a serious hindrance to spiritual growth?*

- *Wiersbe points out that one of the subtle dangers of wealth is a false sense of security. How can a believer best confront that temptation?*

Applying the Truth   *(20 minutes)*

Ask for reactions to this quote from *Be Skillful:* "The real measure of our wealth is how much we'd be worth if we lost all our money." Ask:

- *What does this quote mean to you — in terms of your value in God's eyes?*
- *What Scripture can you cite that supports your claim?*

Say: **We still tend to judge each other by our bank accounts, so let's get practical about this idea of our true worth.** Distribute index cards and ask people to put their best estimate of their financial net worth on the cards (anonymously, and then fold the cards). You can guard privacy by having people use the same marker or pencil. You may also allow those who wish to simply write a question mark. Collect the cards, shuffle them, and redistribute them, saying: **This is your new net worth! How do you like it?** Then ask:

- *Why was it important to us to keep this exercise anonymous?*
- *Look at your card with your "new net worth." How do you feel about having more than, or less than (or not knowing) your actual net worth?*
- *In what ways are all of us here alike, regardless of our differing bank accounts?*

During a moment of silence, read this quote from the bottom of the *Response Sheet:* "**Each of us must discover at what financial level God wants us to live and be content with it.**" Ask people to think (in silence, before your brief closing prayer): **Have you been able to come to acceptance of your financial position in this way? What helps? What hinders?**

ASSIGNMENT

Ask group members to look for newspaper or magazine articles that show the contrast of society's values with biblical values in marriage, family life and parenting, friendships, or neighbor-relations.

FAMILY, FRIENDS, AND NEIGHBORS

TEXT, CHAPTER 8

Session Topic
Applying God's wisdom to our relationships develops our sensitivity to spouse, family members, and friends.

Session Goals
1. To compare and contrast biblical and societal ideas of what makes a good relationship.
2. To explore reasons why society's views about marriage, family, and friendship may be inconsistent with Christian living.
3. To develop prayer topics related to joys and problems in relationships.

Materials Needed
√ Bibles, paper, pencils, index cards
√ Copies of *Be Skillful* for each group member
√ Chalkboard and chalk, or newsprint and markers
√ Two shoe boxes (or other containers), one labeled "Yes" and the other labeled "No."

Special Preparation
1. Optional: Obtain a video clip of 50s or 60s TV family life, for *Launching the Lesson*.
2. Take some time before this session to arrange for three informal interviews of three different generations (for example, interview a grandmother, your spouse, and a teen). Ask these three representatives of the generations: **What does it mean to be a good wife or husband?** Take notes and be ready to comment about the results of your personal survey.

Launching the Lesson

(25 minutes)

Begin by describing the "perfect wife" as portrayed by TV in the 50s and 60s. Ask for volunteers (who are old enough!) to contribute to your description from their memories of watching TV sitcoms in those years. Ask questions like: **How was the role of the wife-mother depicted? How did she dress? How did she relate to her husband and children? What were her main interests? What was her attitude toward life's problems? Why is this vision of the wife and mother so often ridiculed in the media today?**

After this brief discussion, set up a compare-and-contrast exercise by placing *Visual Sketch #3* on the chalkboard.

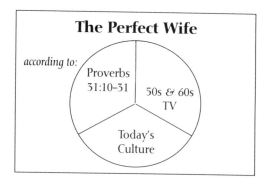

Visual Sketch 3
The Perfect Wife

- *Where do these views of the perfect wife compare, contrast, or overlap?*
- *In your opinion and/or experience, how "realistic" are the views of the perfect wife in each of these three quadrants? Explain.*

OPTIONAL: If possible, instead of merely describing the "perfect wife" of 50s and 60s TV, show a video clip from one of the old TV shows, such as "Donna Reed," "Leave It to Beaver," "Ozzie and Harriet," or "The Dick Van Dyke Show." These shows are full of scenes of the happy wife doing household chores in her dress and high heels.

Discovering God's Principles   *(25 minutes)*

Count off by twos to form two brainstorming teams related to: (1) Biblical Views, and (2) Society's Views. Hand a pencil and numerous index cards to each person on both of the teams. Give everyone about seven minutes to jot down as many entries as possible — one per card — under their team heading, related to biblical or societal views of: Marriage, Family, Friends. Encourage people to review the principles in Proverbs and also the material in *Be Skillful* as they brainstorm. For example, entries might include:

Under Biblical Views
— Marriage is for life
— No divorce
— Parenting by example
— Discipline is a loving practice
— Loyalty a key to friendship

Under Society's Views
— Stay married until love cools
— Schools should do more "parenting"
— Punishment hurts children's self-esteem
— Parents should be good role-models for children
— Use "networking friendships" for career advancement
— True friendship should be valued

At the end of your time limit, gather all the cards and shuffle them. Then place a *Yes* box and a *No* box in front of you. As you read aloud each card, ask the group to vote on: **Could this view possibly be a part of a Christian lifestyle?** Place the card in the appropriate box, based on the majority vote. Then go back and discuss the "no" vote cards. For each one, ask: **Why couldn't this be a Christian approach to marriage, parenting, or friendships? What alternative options might a Christian pursue?** (Note: During the discussion, invite people to share any of the newspaper or magazine clippings they brought to class in response to last week's assignment.)

After drawing this brainstorming activity to a close, follow up with any or all of these discussion questions below. They are based on material presented in the *Be Skillful* chapter:

■ *The book points out that "in ancient days marriages were arranged by the parents." What would you consider to be the benefits and drawbacks of this practice?*

48

- *Why does Wiersbe think that a fifty-fifty approach to marriage is likely to fail? What does he see as a better way, and how does it actually work?*
- *Wiersbe says: "Marriage doesn't change a person's character." What do you think he means by this? Have you found his statement to be true? If so, how?*
- *In what ways have you become aware that the world wants to "kidnap" our children and grandchildren? What can we do about this?*
- *What is your counsel for godly parents whose children rebel against them and against God?*
- *The Wiersbe text states that "it's possible to have many companions and no real friend." What makes a friend more than a companion?*
- *Give a practical example of how a Christian can apply Proverbs 27:6. What is the difference between truth that hurts a friend and truth that harms him or her?*

Applying the Truth   *(10 minutes)*

Place *Visual Sketch #4* on the chalkboard and ask group members to copy it on a sheet of paper. Say: **This grid can serve as a topic-generator for our closing prayer time. Think about possible personal applications of the principles we've discussed today. In which of the areas would you like to praise God for His blessings in your life? In which areas do you see a need for growth or for conflict resolution? Jot some entries, now, in a moment of silence.**

Improving My Relationships

	A PRAISE	A PROBLEM
▶ *Spouse*		
▶ *Children*		
▶ *Friends*		

Visual Sketch 4
Improving My Relationships

After a time of silence, ask people to talk about what they have written. Also let people know that they can simply ask for prayer in one of the areas, without revealing any specific details of the request. Jot concerns as people speak, then close with sentence prayers for one another.

ASSIGNMENT

Ask your group members to prepare for the next session by thinking about: **What situations are you aware of that demonstrate the life-or-death power of words in our world?**

A MATTER OF LIFE OR DEATH

TEXT, CHAPTER 9

Session Topic
Speech is a matter of life or death, and God reminds us that our own words have the power to do great good or harm.

Session Goals
1. To be made aware of the power of words to influence the course of life.
2. To explain the nature and use of speech, according to biblical principles.
3. To identify the words we long to hear from others.

Materials Needed
√ Bibles, paper, pencils, index cards
√ Copies of *Be Skillful* and *Response Sheet #4* for each group member

Special Preparation
Consider doing a brief survey of the word pictures found in the verses quoted in this chapter of *Be Skillful*. Proverbs uses many concrete images to describe the nature of words and speech. Jot a list of the comparisons and contrasts and be ready to refer to them in your comments during the session. (For example: According to Proverbs 26:23, "Fervent lips with a wicked heart are like earthenware covered with silver dross," [NKJV]).

Launching the Lesson   *(12 minutes)*

Open your session with a thought-starter question related to the theme of "words." Ask: **When did a word (or just a few words) make a big difference in your life?** Explain that you are asking about "defining moments" in which a spoken word or phrase had great impact or influence, or changed life's outlook or direction. For example, group members might respond:

— *Inheritance*
— *Not guilty.*
— *It's twins!*
— *We won!* (or: *We lost!*)
— *You owe* (in a letter from the IRS).
— *I'm sorry.*
— *I love you.*
— *Dead* (or: *Alive*)

As a way to get to know one another better, ask people to tell about the circumstances of these life-impacting words. Then discuss:

■ *What kinds of words have been most influential in your life: encouraging words? or hateful-lying words?*
■ *How would you describe the power of words to impact the course of one's life? Would you agree that they are "a matter of life or death"? Explain.*

To make your transition to the next step, say: **In our *Be Skillful* chapter today, Wiersbe tell us: "Never underestimate the power of words." Let's discover some of the biblical principles that make our speech so important to our growth in God's wisdom.**

Discovering God's Principles   *(40 minutes)*

Say: **Imagine—An alien being from outer space has just landed his spaceship in your church parking lot. We go out to investigate and discover that we understand exactly what he wants— though he hasn't said a word to us! He is from the planet Telepath and he wants to know all about this strange phenome-**

non called "speech."

Explain to group members that they are to develop a series of four brief seminars that will inform the curious Telepathian about the nature and use of words and speech: What key instructions would you give our alien—about the nature and use of speech—based on the principles in Proverbs and the material in *Be Skillful*? Also, be sure to include a personal illustration that supports one of the points you would make.

Divide into four groups (related to the four subheads in the text), distribute paper and pencils, and get people started developing their alien-instructing workshops. When the groups are ready, have them present to the whole group what they would tell the alien about words and speech. (Be sure they remember that the Telepathian has never used words! They'll have to explain everything in basic terms.) With your own supplementary comments, help people bring out the main points in *Be Skillful*, referring to key passages in Proverbs.

Bring this step to a close by directing attention to this statement in *Be Skillful:* "The Royal British Navy has a regulation which reads, 'No officer shall speak discouragingly to another officer in the discharge of his duties.' " Discuss: **If this rule were followed perfectly in every Christian congregation, how would it affect our outreach efforts?**

Applying the Truth   *(8 minutes)*

Point out that in the *Launching* portion of this session, you have thought about the impact of words that you have already heard. **But what about the words we hope to hear in the future?**

Distribute copies of *Response Sheet #4* and explain that it can help us think about the words we long to hear from parents, children, a spouse, a friend, or even God. Give people a chance to consider, in silence, what they would like their particular person to say to them.

If people want to jot some words in the letter portion of the sheet, fine. But be sure to let everyone know that they can choose to fill out the *Response Sheet* at home during the week. People may prefer just to think about the words they long for in a few moments of silence before prayer.

Before closing in prayer, say: **The idea of longing for words of healing from others (whether those persons are still living or not), can be an emotionally "heavy" exercise for us. It can,** however, be profoundly healing to the emotions, if we are willing to embrace the grief that surfaces. Some of us will have to grieve and go on with our lives, since the words can never be spoken. This involves coming to a point of acceptance, and such acceptance is healing. Others of us may be able to take actions that will help restore a relationship, perhaps making it possible for long-awaited healing words to be exchanged. May God guide you and bless you as you open up to words of healing in your life.

ASSIGNMENT

Give your group members a TV-watching assignment to prepare themselves for the next session! Ask them to: (1) watch TV shows, news, and sitcoms for any portrayals of Christians; (2) watch the show *Home Improvement* and take notes on its portrayal of family values.

MAKE WAY FOR THE RIGHTEOUS!

TEXT, CHAPTER 10

Session Topic
We must examine our hearts for godly character in order to spread a righteous influence in our world.

Session Goals
1. To discuss the nature of biblical righteousness.
2. To create TV scenes that depict a "realistic" Christian.
3. To examine heart conditions for areas of growth in righteousness.

Materials Needed
√ Bibles, paper, pencils
√ Copies of *Be Skillful* for each group member
√ Chalkboard and chalk, or newsprint and markers
√ Red or pink construction paper; crayons or markers.

Special Preparation
1. Obtain a copy of *Knowledge of the Holy,* by A.W. Tozer (Harper and Row, 1961). Read the chapter on "The Holiness of God" for a devotional background on the first section in this chapter of *Be Skillful* ("The God of Righteousness").
2. Watch the TV show *Home Improvement* at least two or three times before this session. Jot some notes about the show's portrayal of family values—things you could comment about in class.

Launching the Lesson   *(15 minutes)*

Start with an agree-disagree exercise related to the theme of righteousness. Tell group members that you are going to read a series of "controversial" statements. After reading each one, ask for a show of hands indicating whether people agree or disagree with the statement. Then go back and invite people to tell why they responded as they did. Use the suggested discussion questions to make your transition to *Discovering God's Principles*.

1. It's best not to know your level of righteousness.
2. God only gives us commands we are able to keep.
3. To be "justified by faith" requires righteous living.
4. Other religions have some good ideas about how to live right.
5. Hitler may be in heaven.

Discuss:
■ *What is it about "righteousness" that is easy to define? What is hard to define?*
■ *How would you describe a righteous Christian?*

OPTIONAL: Ask your group members to respond to this quote from theologian Anders Nygren, who made the point that it is only because we are lost that salvation is even possible (in *Essence of Christianity*): "Humankind has always dreamed of fellowship with God on the basis of holiness. [Instead], Christianity proclaims fellowship with God on the basis of sin. This is the meaning of the Gospel of Jesus: 'I came not to call the righteous, but sinners.'" After fielding some comments about the quote, ask:

■ *Why is the church often seen as a club for the "good" people, rather than a place for sinners to congregate and encourage one another?*

Discovering God's Principles   *(30 minutes)*

Wiersbe states: "I occasionally hear people lamenting the state of the nation, but most of them fail to point out the main cause: the church collectively, and believers individually, aren't doing their job in spreading righteousness. Ask: **What can we do about this problem?**

After brief discussion, distribute paper and pencils and then focus attention on the third subhead in the *Be Skillful* text: "The Influence of Righteousness." Say: **Most often in our society, especially in the print-media and on TV, Christians are portrayed as legalistic, narrow-minded, and hateful—or as buffoonish caricatures of a truly righteous person. So what would "realistic righteousness"—the kind described in our chapter—look like if it were portrayed accurately on TV?**

Tell your group members that they are going to have the opportunity (working as individuals or partners) to develop a scene in a TV sitcom in which—amazing!—a Christian displays righteousness that reaches out in an effective and biblical way. The scene can involve a circumstance: *(1) in a family setting*, or *(2) in a work setting*, or *(3) in a neighborhood*. Be sure to make this instruction clear: **Be prepared to support your scene-ideas by providing sentences from *Be Skillful* or verses from Proverbs.**

When people are through thinking up their ideas, ask for sharing. Let everyone know they are not expected to have fully developed ideas. The point is simply to contrast the usually warped portrayal with a more biblical portrayal of Christians interacting with others in influential ways.

OPTIONAL: Point out that the TV show *Home Improvement* was influenced by practicing Christians during the development process. Ask:

- *What is your overall impression of* Home Improvement?
- *Do you see any "influence of righteousness" in this show? Explain.*
- *Would you be more, or less, direct about portraying "traditional family values" if you had a chance to write for this show?*

Applying the Truth   *(15 minutes)*

Say: **Wiersbe calls us to "examine our own hearts to make sure we're among the righteous who truly have hope, and that we're the kind of people the Lord can trust with His blessings."**

So invite your group members to give themselves a "heart exam"! Hand out pieces of pink or red construction paper and ask them to tear out a heart-shape. The shape should indicate their sense of their "heart condition" in terms of righteous living—based on the descriptions of righteousness in Proverbs. Then have everyone use a crayon to draw a symbol on their paper hearts according to these options (which you will place on the chalkboard):

- *a lightbulb (symbolizing an ability to understand God's character, and rely on Him)*
- *a shoe (symbolizing the ability to keep walking the path of righteousness by doing good)*
- *a peanut butter jar (symbolizing the ability to spread a righteous influence in the world)*

They will determine which symbol to choose according to what area they believe they need to improve during times of trial. Ask the question this way: **In what areas am I most likely to show "heart trouble" during a stress test?**

Ask volunteers to display their hearts (if they choose) and talk together about everyone's desire for greater righteousness in daily living. Close in prayer.

ASSIGNMENT

Tell your group members that next week they'll be asked to consider (in *Applying the Truth*) how doing God's will is a matter of making the daily choices that come our way. In light of that theme, ask them this week to contemplate this statement by C.S. Lewis: "Total renunciation . . . can mean only a total readiness for every particular renunciation that may be demanded, for it would not be possible to live from moment to moment willing nothing but submission to God as such. What would be the material for the submission?" (*The Problem of Pain*. New York: Macmillan, p. 113.)

Invite people to jot the quote on a piece of paper and think about its practical meaning for them.

ENJOYING GOD'S GUIDANCE

TEXT, CHAPTER 11

Session Topic
Enjoying God's guidance requires developing a life style committed to daily obedience.

Session Goals
1. To discuss the role of hindsight in recognizing God's will.
2. To connect Bible verses to remembered principles of guidance offered in *Be Skillful*.
3. To identify daily choices that strengthen or weaken a relationship with our guiding Lord.

Materials Needed
√ Bibles, paper, pencils
√ Copies of *Be Skillful* for each group member
√ Chalkboard and chalk, or newsprint and markers
√ A hand-mirror

Special Preparation
1. In light of the first sentence in this chapter, do an informal poll during the week. Ask people what comes to mind when they hear the phrase, "will of God." Do this at work or in the neighborhood. If possible, either videotape the responses or audiotape them. At least jot them down so you can share them with the group.
2. In advance, prepare index cards with verse references from Proverbs written on them. Go through the *Be Skillful* chapter and jot down all the Proverbs references. Just jot the numbers on the cards, not the words of the verse, one reference per card. Have the cards ready to hand out during *Discovering God's Principles*.

Launching the Lesson   *(15 minutes)*

OPTIONAL: If you did the informal poll, asking people about the will of God, share some of the responses now. Comment on how peoples' ideas compare and contrast with the biblical concept of God's will.

Gather everyone in a circle and hold up a mirror. State that this is a "hindsight mirror" and that they will each have thirty seconds (or a minute, depending on your groups' size) to hold the mirror over their shoulder and "look back into their past." So doing, they should respond to this question:

■ *When was a time that you know God's will was being accomplished in your life—you can see that now, through hindsight, though your vision was not clear back then?*

Give people a chance to think for a minute, then hand the mirror to the person on your right and let the mirror make it's way around the circle as people respond. Follow up this exercise by asking:

■ *In your opinion, is God's will (when related to an important decision) ever crystal clear at the time? Explain.*

Say: **Today we're going to talk about God's guidance. We'll learn from the Proverbs that enjoying direction from God requires a commitment to developing a daily, intimate communion with Him that results in obedience. In this way, seeking God's will becomes more a matter of choosing to do what pleases Him—because we are so familiar with His character—rather than trying to guess what He might be thinking. Let's find out more.**

Discovering God's Principles   *(25 minutes)*

Write the six numbered subheads from the text on the chalkboard or newsprint, and let everyone know that they will have three minutes to skim the *Be Skillful* chapter silently before you will instruct them to close their books. After the three minutes, hand each person one index card with a verse reference from Proverbs on it (you have already gleaned the references from chapter 11 of the Wiersbe book; see *Special Preparation* above). Say: **Your task is to look up your reference in the Bible and: (1) tell what subhead in *Be Skillful* it relates to and expand on the point of the book section as much as possible, from your memory; (2) tell how you might apply this verse and/or principle to your own life.**

Give people a few minutes to think and perhaps jot some notes before asking them to respond to the rest of the group. Add your own comments and explanations, based on your knowledge of the chapter. If you have time, generate additional discussion with questions like these:

- *Wiersbe states that "unless we see the will of God as the expression of the love of God, we'll resist it." Why do we often think of God's will as something that goes against our plans or our best interests?*
- *How can we begin to see God's will as more loving?*
- *The text makes the point that even the apostle Paul wasn't always sure of the way God was guiding him. He had to do much waiting. When has it been hardest for you to wait for God's leading? In what ways is "waiting on God" an active, rather than a passive, experience?*
- *How do you evaluate the phrase "let go and let God"—in terms of its ability to convey a biblical approach to guidance?*

Applying the Truth   *(20 minutes)*

Now do a quote-reaction activity. (If possible, display this quote on an overhead projector, or photocopy it and hand it out.) C.S. Lewis, the late Christian writer and defender of the faith, wrote in *The Problem of Pain*: "Total renunciation . . . can mean only a total readiness for every particular renunciation that may be demanded, for it would not be possible to live from moment to moment willing nothing but submission to God as such. What would be the material for the submission?" (New York: MacMillan, 1962. p. 113)

Ask: **How does Lewis' view contrast with an approach to God's will that makes it a search for "an answer" to a particular problem or decision?** After some discussion make Wiersbe's point clear: that knowing and doing God's will is a matter of committing our whole lives to God, making daily choices—in obedience to biblical instruction—as they come our way.

Now distribute *Response Sheet #5* and say: **Think about your week past or your week ahead. Jot choices in which you were**

faced with choosing to do or say something that strengthened your relationship to God in one of the six areas or something that weakened or hindered that relationship. Encourage people to be practical and down-to-earth in their responses. Make the point that enjoying God's will simply requires a daily openness to the Spirit's leading in every moment: morning, afternoon, and evening. After people have jotted some responses, ask volunteers to read their responses but don't put undue pressure on anyone. Use the sheets to generate prayer requests and praise of God.

A S S I G N M E N T

Ask people to bring their high school yearbooks to the next session. You will be recalling the "popular sins" of your teen years.

POPULAR SINS

TEXT, CHAPTER 12

Session Topic
Not even Christians are immune to sins that weaken fellowship and threaten the family.

Session Goals
1. To talk about popular sins of our teen years.
2. To develop lectures that convey knowledge about sin.
3. To envision and pray for a renewed church.

Materials Needed
√ Bibles, paper, pencils
√ Copies of *Be Skillful* for each group member
√ Chalkboard and chalk, or newsprint and markers

Special Preparation
To prepare for *Launching the Lesson,* meditate on the descriptions of children found in Proverbs 30:11-14. Think about how these kinds of people might be found in any generation of human history, but consider: In what ways have things gotten qualitatively and quantitatively worse in the last decade?

Launching the Lesson   (10 minutes)

Start by reading aloud this quote from Wiersbe: **"As I read the newspapers and news magazines, I become more and more convinced that we're living in the generation described in Proverbs 30:11-14 with its pride, greed, violence, and lack of appreciation for parents."** Now read Proverbs 30:11-14 aloud and say: **In light of Wiersbe's lament about this generation (and the generations to come), let's recall our own adolescence for a few minutes.** Ask:

- *What were the most "popular sins" in your high school?*
- *How do those sins compare to today's generations' popular sins?*
- *What "lectures" did your parents give you? Are any echoed in our chapter today?*
- *What lecture do you wish you had received, but didn't?*

OPTIONAL: Though "popular sins" is a serious topic, you might start out on a lighter note by having people give some information about themselves as teens—before they respond to the discussion questions. For example, they could reveal their high school nickname, if they had one, and then sing (or say) as much as they remember of their school's fight song or alma mater. This would be a good time to invite "show and tell" with high school yearbooks that people may have brought with them (in response to the assignment from the last session).

Discovering God's Principles   (35 minutes)

Say: **We've thought about how lectures may have helped us when we were growing up and facing the popular sin temptations of our teen years. Now is our chance to work on some lectures to this generation.**

Tell group members that their challenge in this portion of the session is to work as individuals on lectures they might give to a crowd of teens. Ask them to imagine standing at a high school assembly and speaking on the topic: "Popular Sins."

Hand out paper and pencils for jotting notes, assign each person one of the five subheads in *Be Skillful*, and tell people to structure their comments around these two outline headings (written on the chalkboard):

—What you need to know about this sin
—How I've learned my own lesson with this sin

Encourage people to be anecdotal in their sharing about how they would attempt to communicate with young people about sin. Then discuss together:

- *What types of criticisms, challenges, or questions do you think you might receive from the audience?*
- *Is there really any way to "lecture" young people without turning them off? What ideas do you have?*
- *What changes would you make in a lecture to today's secular adults? Christian adults?*

After some discussion of the questions above, follow up with these questions, as time allows:

- *Wiersbe states that popular sins are "weakening our homes, threatening the peace of our communities, and destroying our lives." What is the main "threat" in your community? To your home?*
- *Explain the author's rationale for total abstinence from strong drink. What personal guidelines do you have for "playing it safe" with alcohol?*
- *In your opinion, are children more, or less, respectful today than in generations past? How would you support your contention?*
- *Many people today "enjoy riches and fame vicariously as they follow the career of their favorite celebrity." What are some of the sad consequences of this approach to life? How does Matthew 7:24-29 speak to the problem?*
- *How is covetousness like cancer? Give a practical example.*
- *Explain what preacher James Denney meant when he said: "No man can give the impression that he himself is clever and that Christ is mighty to save."*

Applying the Truth   (15 minutes)

Direct attention to this statement near the end of Wiersbe's chapter: "We expect to find these sins prevalent among lost people, but we don't expect to find them in the church. If the church ever hopes to witness to the lost world, it must be different from the lost world."

Have everyone look at the five short paragraphs that follow this quote, in which Wiersbe gives examples of early-church sinfulness. Spend some time reading through the Scripture passages given in these paragraphs. Then ask: **In what ways would you say that the same, or similar, problems affect the Christian church today?**

Spend the rest of your time together sharing visions for a renewed church — the church at large and the local church or churches of your group. Close with an extended prayer time based on the issues you raise in your sharing.

OPTIONAL: If it would not prove to be too threatening in your situation, you could make this last step into a practical problem-solving exercise, directly related to problems in your local congregation. Be sure to lead the brainstorming in a non-judgmental way. Don't focus on particular personalities. Just try to generate solutions to forms of "sinfulness" to which all members seem to contribute.

ASSIGNMENT

Ask your group members to come to the next session prepared to talk about what your course — and the group's fellowship — has meant to them during the past weeks. Give them these questions to ponder: **What personal insights or learnings have been especially significant for you? In what ways have we grown in fellowship with one another?**

Also ask people to think about their desires for the future of the group. What would they like to do next: keep studying together? Take a break? Add new people? Ask people to be ready to share their suggestions next time.

"THIS GOD IS OUR GOD"

TEXT, CHAPTER 13

Session Topic

As we grow in knowledge of who our God is, we grow in our ability to live wisely and skillfully.

Session Goals

1. To display impressions of who God is.
2. To highlight information in the text by playing a "Jeopardy" game.
3. To identify personal applications related to God's attributes.

Materials Needed

√ Bibles, paper, pencils
√ Copies of *Be Skillful* for each group member, and copies of *Response Sheet #6*
√ Chalkboard and chalk, or newsprint and markers
√ A large piece of newsprint or butcher paper; sheets of construction paper; paste

Special Preparation

1. A good way to prepare for this chapter on God's nature would be to read from the book *Your God Is Too Small*, by J.B. Phillips (Macmillan, 1971). Phillips gives wonderful descriptions of "unreal gods" and "an adequate God."
2. Prepare the graffiti poster in advance, as described in *Launching the Lesson*. Also consider making up more answers for the "Skillful Jeopardy Game," as many as you wish, depending on your time limitations.

Launching the Lesson   *(10 minutes)*

Begin with a graffiti-poster activity. In advance, write the words "OUR GOD IS . . ." in the center of a large piece of newsprint (or butcher paper) and tape it to a wall. As people enter the room, direct them to the poster and a box of crayons or bright-colored markers. Also make available sheets of construction paper and paste.

As they arrive, ask your group members to think: **What immediately comes to mind when you hear the word "God"? How could you picture your reaction in living color?** Their task is to mark the poster with a creative piece of graffiti that shows their initial response to "God." They could make a drawing, a symbol, a word, a phrase, a picture — anything that would convey the impact (past or present) of this word on them. If they wish, they could tear pieces of the construction paper and paste them to the poster. Tell people that you hope the end result will be a colorful display of this group's experience of who God is for them.

When everyone has had a chance to participate, point to this quote from A.W. Tozer in the text: "The essence of idolatry is the entertainment of thoughts about God that are unworthy of Him." Say: **This is a serious statement! Look at the ways we have pictured our God. In your opinion, how accurate is our depiction?**

After discussing for a moment, follow up with these questions:

- *What attributes of God are most important to you? Why?*
- *How have you experienced these attributes "in action" in your daily life?*

Discovering God's Principles   *(25 minutes)*

Say: **For our session today, we've read in** *Be Skillful* **about four of the attributes of our God that come through in Proverbs. How much have you learned from this chapter? How much do you remember? Let's find out!** Have some fun while bringing out some key concepts in *Be Skillful*, chapter 13 by playing "Skillful Jeopardy Game." Here's how it works: First, divide into two teams and decide on a "buzzer" system (either standing up, raising hands, or making two different noises; you may need someone to watch for who responds first). Then have everyone quickly skim the chapter before closing their books for the game. (Note: Instruct people to close their Bibles before each question, but let them know that they may look up verses when questions deal with Bible text information.)

To play the game, read aloud the answers below and ask your group members to come up with the questions (given in parentheses). If your group enjoys competition, set up a scoring system, and even offer a small prize for the winning team. Be sure to allow time between game-answers for comments, questions, or discussion themes that may be raised.

Answers and Questions:

—From the Latin words *video* and *pro,* it's more than just "foreseeing." (What is *providence?*)

—If we weren't in a universe, we'd likely be in this. (What is a *"multiverse."*)

—He said: "Life can only be understood backward, but it must be lived forward." (Who is *Kierkegaard?*)

—Along with oppression, it's possible to sin against the poor this way too. (What is *neglect?*)

—It's an English translation of a Hebrew word meaning "utterly different" (What is *holy?*)

—The ancient Israelites used them like fences. (What are *stones?*)

—These are folks God will defend, as a lawyer, according to Proverbs 23:10-11. (Who are the *fatherless?*)

—According to A.T. Piersons, this is what history really is. (What is *His story?*)

—It was ancient Israel's equivalent of our modern courtroom. (What was *the gate?*)

—A stimulus to evangelism, rather than a deterrent. (What is God's *sovereignty?*)

—These are the kind of eyes God hates, according to Proverbs 6:17. (What are *haughty* eyes?)

—It's a Greek way to say that Jesus is the beginning and end. (What is *alpha and omega?*)

—Along with decreeing the end, God decrees this too. (What is *the means?*)

Wrap up this step with a summarizing statement and a key question: **The key point of this chapter is that as we grow in intimacy with God, we grow in our ability to live skillfully. What will it take for you to become better acquainted with God in the coming year?**

Applying the Truth *(25 minutes)*

Now distribute copies of *Response Sheet #6* to everyone. Say: **We know what God is like only because He has chosen to reveal Himself to us. Yet none of us can say we have a complete "handle" on God's nature, since God is infinite, and our minds are only finite. The Bible, however, tells us we can have a picture in mind when we think of God: We can recall the person of Jesus, who was God on earth, in flesh and blood.**

Invite people to consider the four aspects of God's character as revealed in the life of Jesus Christ. Then ask them to choose one or more of those aspects and apply them to their lives in specific ways. Have them jot some notes in the blanks provided and be ready to share those personal applications with the rest of the group before a closing prayer.

Building the Body

Since this is your last session of the course, have a special form of "closure." For example, you might simply ask people to think about what this course and their time together has meant to them. Say: **Think back through the course in your minds. What personal insights or learnings come to mind as being especially significant for you? In what ways have we grown in fellowship with one another? What affirmations would you like to share with one another?**

If possible, offer some refreshments and spend some time in fellowship. Some groups may wish to continue with another study book. Others may want to take a break for a while before starting up again in the future. Still other groups may plan to do some outreach — seek to bring new people into the group — before starting up again. Be sure to cover these issues together and firm up your plans for the future of your group before everyone leaves for home.

Notes

Notes